CW00408126

6 721 724 000

A BOOT UP

THE SOUTH WEST COAST PATH

SOUTH CORNWALL

Philip Carter

First published in Great Britain in 2010

Copyright text and photographs © 2010 Philip Carter

All rights reserved. No part of this publication may be reproduced, stored in a retrieval system, or transmitted in any form or by any means without the prior permission of the copyright holder.

British Library Cataloguing-in-Publication Data
A CIP record for this title is available from the British Library

ISBN 978 0 85710 013 9

PiXZ Books
Halsgrove House, Ryelands Industrial Estate,
Bagley Road, Wellington, Somerset TA21 9PZ
Tel: 01823 653777
Fax: 01823 216796
email: sales@halsgrove.com

An imprint of Halstar Ltd, part of the Halsgrove group of companies
Information on all Halsgrove titles is available at: www.halsgrove.com

Printed and bound in China by Toppan Leefung Printing Ltd

Contents

How to use this book

The South West Coast Path offers all things to all people. For those who require a real challenge there are 630 miles (1014 km) of continuous path some of it rugged indeed. However, other parts are entirely flat and make for the easiest of walking. Whatever your choice it is hoped that this little selection will give you pleasure and maybe items of interest as well. The 'level' shown near the beginning of each walk is an indication of the exertion required. 🍂 🍂 🍂 will take more effort than 🍂 🍂 and 🍂 🍂 than 🍂 .

The waymark for the Coast Path, as it is indeed for all official long distance trails or footpaths, is a single upright acorn. So if you are in doubt as to whether you are on or off the path - look for the acorn. Having said that be careful as the National Trust use a spray of acorns as a symbol and some of the Coast Path belongs to them. Therefore you can find stretches with both. But as stated at the outset if you have a single upright acorn you are on the Coast Path.

In this series there is a selection of short, mostly circular walks, taking in parts of the Coast Path. Because they are mostly circular they can of course be walked in reverse. However, they are devised to save the best views until last so it is suggested you try them first as described. To give more opportunities of access and to vary the terrain and experience the walks chosen are spread along the coast. The one thing that they all have in common is a high scenic value. None of them are dull and many incorporate short stretches of the best the Coast Path has to offer.

Remember too the origin of this Coastal Path was as a walking route for revenue men patrolling to prevent smuggling. This meant that the path had to hug the coastline. The revenue men had to be able to see the end of

every headland and look into each creek and inlet.

Some walks pass places of refreshment others do not. But you are always well advised to carry a flask and a little something to eat. The views are never quite so good if you are hungry!

Undoubtedly the very best time to walk is the late spring when the coastal flowers are at their best. Having said that more people walk in summer than any other time and some walks are best when the autumn colours are in evidence. Go well shod with footwear that has a grip as this will make even the hardest walk easier.

Whatever time you pick to walk and whatever area you choose you can be assured there will always be something of interest to engage the mind. The coast has for centuries been a working place and old mills, fish cellars and limekilns bear this out. The coastline too has often in times of conflict been our first line of defence so much remains to remind you of wars in the past.

These walks provide a taste of what the Coast Path has to offer. If you get hooked the best source of further information is The South West Coast Path Association. They publish an updated annual guide as well as a set of Path Descriptions covering the whole path. They are also happy to

answer specific enquiries. Contact the South West Coast Path Association (Registered Charity Number 266754) Bowker House, Lee Mill Bridge, Ivybridge, Devon, PL21 9EF
Telephone: 01752 896237
Fax: 01752 893654
E-mail info@swcp.org.uk Web site www.swcp.org.uk

The South Cornwall coast is generally regarded as being softer than the North coast and parts of it are more remote from the usual tourist run. However, you may doubt the veracity of either statement in some of these walks. There are walks not without exertion and others which are so deservedly attractive that at times they are busy with fellow walkers.

Key to Symbols Used

Level of difficulty:

Easy

Fair

More challenging

Map symbols:

🚗 Park & start

—— Tarred Road

- - - - Footpath

■ Building / Town

+ Church

🍺 Pub

Walk Locations

ATLANTIC OCEAN

CORNWALL

LISKARD •

PLYMOUTH
10

FOWEY
• 8

ST AUSTELL •
7

9
Rame
Head

FALMOUTH •
6 Dodman
Point

4 5

PENZANCE
•

1 2

3
Lizard
Point

ATLANTIC OCEAN

1 Treen – Porthcurno – Penberth

This Treen, near St Buryan in the south of Penwith, should not be confused with the other Treen near Zennor the north of Penwith.

A walk that takes you to some interesting places on the south Cornish coast.

Only a short walk but you can add to the exercise by going up to see the Minack Theatre or out to take a closer look at Treryn Dinas and the Logan Rock. This is granite country which means stone stiles and sometimes rocky paths.

Level 🐚 🐚
Length three miles (4.8 km.)
Start Treen car park 385 225 this is not the first car park you come to in Treen.
OS Map Explorer 102 Land's End
Refreshments at both Treen and Porthcurno.

Treryn Dinas from the Minack.

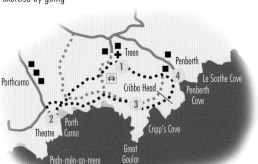

Map showing: Porthcurno, Treen, Penberth, Le Scathe Cove, Penberth Cove, Cribba Head, Theatre, Porth Curno, Cripp's Cove, Great Goular, Pedn-mên-an-mere. Points marked 1, 2, 3, 4.

1000 m

① Do not be beguiled by foot-path sign next to car park which says 'Penberth only' as this is correct. Walk back out of the car park to turn left, very soon there is a sign forward to Treen Cliff. The road becomes a track and you pass into a camping site. Pass left of an ablution block and go forward and right. About halfway along the site is a stone stile going left, take this. In the first field cross to the far corner, in the next field go diagonally again but not as far as the far corner. The third field is still crossed diagonally but thereafter you keep by right hedge until you exit into an enclosed path. After a few yards turn right and after a further few yards keep ahead although the Coast Path goes left. The path descends into the Porthcurno valley; turn left when you reach the track. Shortly you again reach the Coast Path signified by a squat stone marker.

Porthcurno is well known far beyond its boundaries for two things: as a cable station and for the open air Minack Theatre. The first cable was laid in the 1870s including one to what was then Bombay (now Mumbai), the first

At the Minack Theatre.

long distance cable in the British Empire. The earliest across the Atlantic was laid in 1880. The number of cables to different destinations here grew to about twenty. However, technology advanced and the old telegraph cables have been replaced by fewer modern fibre-optic ones. There was even a special school here to train operators but this was closed in 1994. In World War II operations were transferred underground and the tunnels now serve as a Museum of Telegraphy. The Minack Theatre was started by Miss Rowena Cade in 1935. It had humble beginnings but has flourished over the years and now every summer puts on a varied programme. Names and dates of productions over the years are inscribed on the concrete seats.

(2) This is decision time. If you have never seen the Minack Theatre proceed right and west along the Coast Path signed 'Porth Gwarra' along the west side of the cove and climb the long flight of steep steps to get to the theatre. To bypass it turn left and East along the Coast Path. However, we suggest first going the few yards forward to look down to the magnificently coloured cove.

The Coast Path climbs steeply uphill and at the top a short spur path goes right to a war time block house and viewpoint. The main path goes left and shortly you are back to the point you left the Coast Path earlier. Here turn right. Ignore an unmarked path going left but at the next Coast Path sign there is an unmarked path going

Aerial view of the Minack Theatre.

right, take this. It is a much more scenic route and passes a white pyramid with a plaque telling of cable history. Presently a path forks right going down to the beach here keep left and the loop path comes back to

the Coast Path by a stone seat. There bear sharp right to soon pass through a kissing gate. Later a track joins from left, continue forward. Then soon a path joins from left and you come to a footpath fork.

Percella Point.

(3) Decision time again as the right fork takes you out to Treryn Dinas and if you are agile you can climb the Logan Rock. This is only a short out and return. The left fork beside the one time earth bank of the cliff castle is the path on to Penberth.

The headland of Treryn Dinas is another of the Iron Age cliff castles, the most famous feature of which is the Logan Rock. This enormous perhaps sixty ton granite boulder was so delicately poised that it used to rock. Log is a Cornish word meaning that. However a naval Lieutenant Hugh Goldsmith, nephew of the poet Oliver Goldsmith, dislodged it as a prank. There was an outcry from the locals sufficient to stir the Admiralty to insist the Lieutenant restore it. At considerable expense to himself, the

Dodder a parasite on Gorse.

use of tackle and many men the stone was put back but it never rocked again as well as formerly.

(4) You will almost certainly wish to explore Penberth but then return to where you arrived and proceed up the track you first joined. This passes right of a house and becomes a footpath, unsigned at present. You pass parallel privet hedges evidence of one time flower growing. You enter a wood and shortly fork left to go uphill on a sometimes

Porthcurno from the Logan Rock.

stepped path through trees. There are several woodland paths which lead off off but the main route is fairly obvious. At the top there is a stile into a field. Keep along right hedge. In the next field start with left hedge but when you get to a kink go forward and slightly right to come to a gate at the top of the field. Keep on by left hedge for about twenty yards to cross another stile into a wired in path which goes round to Treen car park.

Penberth.

Fishing boat at Penberth.

Penberth is still an active fishing community but the number of working boats is, as elsewhere, now much reduced. The object which catches most eyes is the former manually operated capstan for hauling boats ashore. This is now done mechanically but the National Trust have restored and preserved the original capstan. The boats have 'PZ' which designates Penzance as their registration letter. • This was once a great area for growing early flowers such as violets, narcissi and daffodils, and many of the hedges planted as shelter breaks remain.

2 Lamorna – Mousehole

A walk among old quarries, farmland and coast.

A walk with refreshment at both ends should surely have something to recommend it!

This walk gives a sight of coastline granite but the best is saved until towards the end. Warning: because this is granite country there are lots of stone stiles and often stony paths.

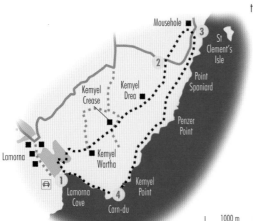

Level 👢 👢
Length just over five miles (8 km.)
Park at Lamorna Cove 450 241.
OS Map Explorer 102 Land's End
Refreshments at both Lamorna Cove and Mousehole.

Day fading near Lamorna.

① Walk back from the car park to pick up the Coastal Path going right and East. It is a road passing in front of a row of houses. It soon arrives at a bridge then becomes a path mostly concrete curving uphill. Just round the first bend leave the Coast Path for a footpath going left, no sign but it is waymarked. The path takes a sinuous route uphill through long discontinued quarries with occasional views seaward. At the top a footpath joins from the left but you bear right. The path soon becomes a track go forward past buildings, Kemyel Warth, to take a stone stile on your right.

The stile leads into fields with distant views of the West coast of the Lizard. The path in the third field goes across

Celtic Cross at Kemyel Drea.

diagonally to an ingenious stile in the corner. The path is for a short while a lane then a road, go forward past buildings, Kemyel Crease, to another stone stile on your right,. The path soon becomes enclosed and can be mucky in wet weather. It turns into a track and you cross a road to go

through a series of pedestrian gates and a farmyard, Kemyel Drea.

Note the little cross beside the path. The path keeps by the left hedge through two fields and then goes across the middle of the third towards buildings, Raginnis.

2 The path exits into a road, turn right and almost immediately bear left. The road becomes a track then a grassy lane but eventually there is another stone stile on your right, take this. In the fourth field there is a footpath fork go right to come down to a gate and steps down to a drive. Turn left and in a few yards right there is only an arrow in an old may tree to guide you. Go down a

The harbour at Mousehole.

Mousehole was once of more importance than Newlyn or Penzance. The Spaniards raided here in 1595 and not only torched the place but went on to destroy Newlyn and Penzance. Nettie Pender, a local historian has written of her early recollections there. Interesting reading it is too, highlighting as it does how much times have changed even within living memory. Off shore is St Clement's Isle, there was once a small chapel there dedicated to that particular saint, because he was the patron saint of sailors. Dylan Thomas the Welsh writer found the place lovely having spent his honeymoon here. Mousehole these days has received publicity from the children's story The Mousehole Cat and is known for its display of Christmas lights.

Bantam at Mousehole Bird Hospital.

At the end of the terrace turn right up a hill and then fork slightly right to go up again. Here turn left up the main road, avoid footpath going left to continue up, passing the Bird Hospital. Finally at the top of the hill the road goes right but the Coast Path goes left signed 'Lamorna 2 miles'. Unfortunately here for a while the route is a dull lane away from the sea whereas the old coastguard path with

path beside a stream, ignore private path on right and railed path going left. At the bottom you are facing a cottage, turn right and then left. In a few yards right again to go down steps, which lead to a road with a kink which comes out opposite the war memorial by the harbour.

3 At the harbour turn right along the road this is the Coast Path. Shortly take a left fork Keigwin Place, to come opposite Keigwin Manor. Here turn left and then right keeping along harbour side and then in front of a terrace which has small gardens to left of the road.

The Bird Hospital here is now an independent charity but was originally founded by the Yglesias sisters one of whom wrote The Cry of a Bird. *• The name Point Spaniard recalls the Spanish raid of 1595.*

its stone stiles was far below. The path passes inland of Point Spaniard. After a while there is the long descent to eventually get back to a coastal route. The path passes through a pine wood, at the Wildlife Trust notice keep

Mousehole Bird Hospital.

left to come out close to the Carn-du headland.

(4) From Carn-du the dramatic rocky path makes its way along the eastern side of Lamorna Cove. The view is fine but you do need to watch where you are putting your feet!

Lamorna is a place that has changed much over the years. Originally it was a small fishing port then it became a major quarrying area and has now reverted to a small holiday resort.

Dartmoor had been a major source of granite in past centuries but it had to be taken to the coast to be shipped. Here at Lamorna it was already on the coast, so costs were less. In

Keigwin Manor, Spanish raid survivor

1834-5 a pier was built to facilitate loading; quarrying ceased in 1910. A lot of stone for building the Thames Embankment came from here as well as material for the Wolf and Bishop's Rock lighthouses.

Lamorna Cove, once a quarrying centre.

3 **The Lizard**

A delightful walk to England's most southerly point.

A walk around England's most southerly point, much of interest with some wonderful scenery. The area because of its geology of serpentine rock and mild climate has a flora all its own. Furthermore you may be lucky enough to see a Cornish chough.

There is less climbing than on many coastal walks but some effort will be expended.

Level 🐾 🐾
Length just over four and a half miles (7.2 km.)
Start at large car park at Lizard Town* 703 612. *the OS omits 'town' but it carries on regardless of the OS!.
OS Map Explorer 103 The Lizard
Refreshments you are spoilt for choice; plenty at Lizard Town the start and finish. A specialist pasty shop very soon after the start and an upswept hotel above Housel Bay then a choice of cafes near Polpeor Cove about half way round.

Crane Ledges

Lizard

Hotel

The Balk

Hot Point

Lighthouse

Bass Point

Coastguard Station

Lizard Point

Housel Bay

Vellan Drang

1000 m

Kilcobben Cove lifeboat house.

1 Take the road east signposted Church Cove, presently there is a right fork signed Church Cove, take this, pass the church, and go down the road to Church Cove.

Landewednack Church, is the most southerly parish church in the country, and is dedicated to St Winwallo (various spellings). It is very ancient although there is disagreement about just how old it is. Church Cove was once involved in pilchard fishing.

2 At Church Cove turn right on the Coast Path. Shortly pass Kilcobben Cove and proceed round Bass Point passing the Marconi Museum and the old Lloyd's signal station to Housel Bay. Do not miss the Lion's Den collapsed cave just before

the lighthouse. There is no sign but where the path takes a right-angled turn at end of a wall divert a few yards down to the left by a notice saying Crumbling Cliff. There is plenty of opportunity for refreshment where the road comes down to Polpeor Cove.

Lion's Den collapsed cave.

The lifeboat station was moved to Kilcobben in 1961 from Polpeor Cove to be in a less exposed situation. • The Marconi Museum is on the site used by Marconi for the early experimental reception of messages from the Isle of Wight. Lloyd's Signal station was used to send messages to ships. In the days before modern communication ships on long voyages were often directed to go to the Lizard for orders. They would then be directed to the port where the commodities they were carrying would fetch the best prices. • The Lion's Den is a sea cave where the roof has fallen in. • Lighthouses have a long history on the Lizard, the first was built in 1619 erected by Sir John Killigrew. Trinity House set up their's in 1781 and at one time it was the most powerful lighthouse in the world. It was automated in 1998.

(3) Continue west passing Pistol Meadows, you are now in chough country to reach Lizard Point where you turn North. There are several paths and tracks back to Lizard Town but the one suggested is from Caerthillian Cove. As you go north from Lizard Point you cross two small streams in succession, then go up steps and there is a marker post pointing left for Coast Path but is the right hand path signed with blue arrow that you want.

(4) Take this bridleway which presently crosses a bridge. On your way back there are two signed footpaths right and unsigned one left but continue uphill with the worn bridleway that later becomes a lane to the car park.

Lloyds signal station.

Pistol Meadows was another place where drowned sailors were buried until legislation allowed them to be interred in local churchyards. • Choughs, the Cornish emblem with their characteristic tumbling flight, are now back nesting and breeding in Cornwall after an absence of about fifty years. • Many people mistake the area close to Polpeor Cove as the Lizard but the true Lizard Point is half a mile West.

At the true Lizard Point.

4 Falmouth, Swanpool – Maenporth

A short but scenic walk to the outskirts of Falmouth.

Despite its nearness to urban Falmouth this walk is relatively rural and there are extensive views across Falmouth Bay

A brief walk with two hills the first is the steeper.

A walk that is out and back but the return route is varied.

FALMOUTH
Swanpool
1
Pennance Point
Sunny Cove
2
Falmouth Bay
3
Maenporth

1000 m

Level 🥾 but there is one noticeable hill.
Length just over three miles (4.8 km.).
Start Swanpool car park at the western end of Falmouth 801 313
OS Map Explorer 103 The Lizard. Part of the route is on 105 Falmouth.
Refreshments seasonal at Swanpool and for a longer period at Maenporth.

① The car park is at the southern end of Swan Pool, walk towards the sea and turn right up the road. After a very few yards turn left on to the Coast Path. At first there is a rail fence on your right, a couple of yards after it ends there is a stile on your right. Go over this and proceed uphill alongside the right hedge. There is a diagonal path across the field but this is NOT the one you want. At the top right corner of the field is a stone stile. Look back at the view. The path then crosses a golf course sometimes open sometimes

Wreck 1979 Ben Asdale *from Aberdeen.*

Swanpool derives its name from its former use by the important local Killigrew family for breeding swans.

enclosed. The last enclosed section has a well signed left turn and comes down to the Coast Path.

② Here turn right and continue along and mostly downhill on the Coast Path down to Maenporth,

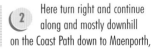

where refreshment is usually available.

(3) Then return the way you came but this time stay on the Coast Path the whole way. In so doing you will pass the site of the wreck of the *Ben Asdale*, and the Home Guard monument on Pennance Point. Later there is an unmarked stile on your right, do not take it but stay with the main path. Shortly after this you pass the stile on the left you took on your outward trip and come again back to the road above the car park.

South West Coast footpath sign at Maenporth.

Home Guard memorial Pennance Point.

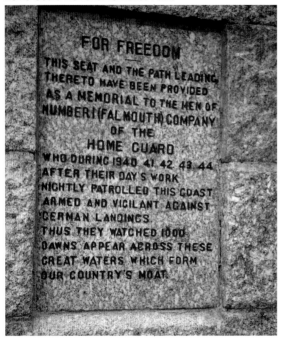

FOR FREEDOM

THIS SEAT AND THE PATH LEADING
THERETO HAVE BEEN PROVIDED
AS A MEMORIAL TO THE MEN OF
NUMBER I (FALMOUTH) COMPANY
OF THE
HOME GUARD
WHO DURING 1940 41 42 43 44
AFTER THEIR DAY'S WORK
NIGHTLY PATROLLED THIS COAST
ARMED AND VIGILANT AGAINST
GERMAN LANDINGS
THUS THEY WATCHED 1000
DAWNS APPEAR ACROSS THESE
GREAT WATERS WHICH FORM
OUR COUNTRY'S MOAT.

The Ben Asdale was an Aberdeen trawler supplying fish to a Russian factory ship. The trawler went ashore in a storm in 1979 causing a difficult helicopter rescue. • On Pennance Point a short distance before Falmouth is a memorial to the men of the local Home Guard who 'after the day's work nightly patrolled this coast armed and vigilant against German landings thus they watched a thousand dawns appear across these great waters which form our country's moat'. • Close by was an old lead mine that was converted in 1875 into an arsenic works. For about 15 years it was busy exporting arsenic mostly to the USA as a pest control for the cotton boll weevil.

5 **St Anthony's Head**

A lighthouse an ancient house and a beautiful beach.

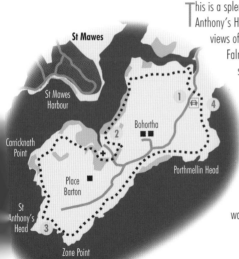

This is a splendid walk around St Anthony's Head giving extensive views of St Mawes and Falmouth. An alternative start could be made from St Mawes by using the seasonal ferry to Place.

There is some climbing but the walk is less arduous than much coastal walking.

1000 m

Level 🐾 🐾

Length is a little over six miles (9.6-km).

Park Porth Farm National Trust car park 867 329

OS Map Explorer 105 Falmouth & Mevagissey

Refreshments none but Portscatho is not far away.

Spectacular landscape near St Anthony's Head.

St Mawes seen across the water.

Froe was a one time tidal mill of which there were a number in this area. They were environmentally friendly but very hard graft to maintain and operate because the work pattern was dictated by the ever-changing tides.

(1) There are actually two parts to the car park at Porth. The lower one is better because the path actually starts from there. The sign says 'Place', the path goes down to and then follows Porth Creek and later down the Percuil River. Early on there are views across to Froe. There are several paths signed inland to Bohortha ignore them all. You pass the Old lower ferry landing point to arrive at a road at Place.

(2) At the road turn left though the unhelpful sign has its back to you. You now follow the Coast Path signs, go up the road passing the entrance to Place House. Shortly turn right, but watch for the Coast Path sign as it is not well-positioned, and go past the old church. The path for a while is sinuous but well way-marked except when you

St Anthony's Lighthouse.

come down to a track where there is no sign to tell you to turn left. Then simply follow the Coast Path all the way round to St Anthony's Head. On your way there you go through an attractive pine wood, pass a little dam, a fuel store and have the opportunity to walk out to the lighthouse. This is all before ascending steeply to St Anthony's Head.

Falmouth from St Anthony's Head.

Place Manor.

③ At St Anthony's head pause to admire the view then continue along the Coast Path. You pass N.T. signs for Porthbeor and Killigerran before you reach Towan Beach.

The views from the head are magnificent, particularly look across Falmouth Harbour, the Carrick Roads as it is called to Pendennis Castle above and to the left of Falmouth Docks. The National Trust holiday

Place was originally the site of an Augustinian priory, it later became a manor house and after that for a while a hotel. The lawn in front was once the pond for another tidal mill and this one was reputed to have run for three hundred years. John Leland, 'king's antiquary' to King Henry VIII observed the mill in 1538. • The ancient church is dedicated to St Anthony and Pevsner wrote of it that it was the best example in Cornwall of what a church used to look like.
• The dam was to provide water for the gun battery on St Anthony's Head before it was connected to mains water. The fuel store was for the lighthouse and the fuel had to be carried there. The lighthouse was constructed in 1834/5 and was automated in 1987.

lets were part of the buildings for the battery on St Anthony's Head that was begun in 1885 and up-graded in 1898. It was rearmed at the beginning of World War II and stayed in military occupation until 1956.

(4) At Towan Beach you come down to a track with a blue arrow bridle way sign pointing left that also says 'Porth Farm car park'. This is the way you want, so leave the Coast Path here and walk up to the car park.

View of Falmouth at sunset.

There used to be an annual challenge walk of 33 miles along the Southern Cornish Coast from St Anthony's Head to St Austell. Those who could accomplish the tough course in twelve hours were rewarded with a pasty and a cup of tea! • Scabious is so called because it was considered to be a cure for scabies. It was once used by a possibly extinct species, indecisive young ladies, to determine - he loves me he loves me not? • Towan is the Cornish word for sand dune so presumably there were some in days gone by, but they have gone now.

Towan Beach, across Porth Creek towards St Mawes.

6 The Dodman

A rewarding walk off the beaten track.

This walk is in a remote part of southern Cornwall but is mostly fine high level walking,

This headland walk is short and in clear weather provides considerable views, some even regard it as the best viewpoint on the South coast of Cornwall. However the snag is that you have to get up on to the headland first and it is some climb!

Level 🌱 🌱 🌱
Length two and a half miles (4 km.)
Park at Penare car park 999 404
OS Map Explorer 105 Falmouth & Mevagissey
Refreshments none on the walk, but Gorran Haven is not too far away.

Bow or Vault Beach

Hemmick Beach

Penare Farm

Gell Point

Penveor Point

Carlithey Point

Dodman Horse

The Bell

Dodman Point

1000 m

Cornish herring-bone walling

Hemmick Beach

① From Penare car park walk back out of the entrance to pick up the footpath opposite going westwards roughly parallel to the road to Hemmick Beach. Presently you are directed up steps and asked to keep close to the fence. Just before you reach the coast by the end of a section of rail fence there is a narrow path forking left, if you take this you save a little of the climb to come.

② At the Coast Path turn left and ascend the steep hill and it really is steep at the start, there are then a couple of dips and a longer less steep hill to gain the high level peninsula, known as the Dodman. Look westwards, across Veryan Bay for views of Gull Rock off Nare Head and beyond. Pass by a footpath running inland signed 'Penare' along 'The Bulwark' to come out close to the southern tip, of the headland, here divert a few yards right to view the cross.

The Dodman from West Portholland.

3 Retrace steps to Coast Path, where you may if you wish divert to see the Watch House. Continue along the path then proceed up the other side of the headland.

Look East for views of Vault Beach, the Gwinges Rocks off Gorran Haven and even distant views of the 'Cornish Alps'. Continue until you are abreast of Penover Point

Memorial cross on the Dodman.

and reach the other end of 'The Bulwark'.

Dodman is a corruption of 'deadman' perhaps of some shipwreck of long ago. The peninsula was an Iron Age fort and 'The Bulwark;' was the earthwork that provided the landward side defence. The cross is a memorial to the destroyers HMS Lynx and Thrasher wrecked here in 1896. The local vicar who was responsible for having the cross erected hoped it would in part act as a daymark to warn other shipping.

4 Turn left and upwards to take the path along 'The 'Bulwark' signed Penare 1/3 M.' (Do not get excited about how close you are as the next sign will still show same distance!) Presently fork right signed 'Penare' to pick up a lane running back to Penare and the car park.

The Watch House was built in 1795 and was one of a chain of signal stations built by the Admiralty to give advance news of shipping movements to the Navy at Plymouth. • 'Q', Sir Arthur Quiller Couch used the Dodman as the setting in his book Dead Man's Rock. Bell heather grows here. • The 'Cornish Alps' as they are called are really the spoil heaps from china clay workings in the St Austell area.

Bell Heather.

St Mawes Harbour, with the town on the left and the Percuil River beyond. In the mid distance Nare Head and Gull Rock and farther The Dodman.

7 Fowey, the Gribbin

A superb headland walk with much of interest en route.

The walk especially the coastal section is pleasant enough but in addition there are items of interest to beguile the mind.

This walk starts inland but then circumvents the high level route of the Coast Path around the Gribbin Peninsula.

The dramatic red and white daymark dominates Gribben Head.

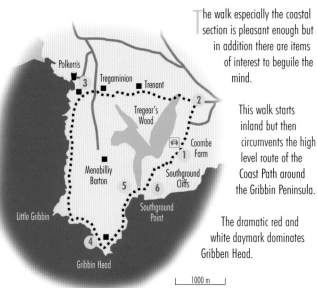

Polkerris

Tregaminion   Trenant

Tregear's Wood

Coombe Farm

Menabilliy Barton

Southground Cliffs

Little Gribbin

Southground Point

Gribbin Head

1000 m

Level 🥾🥾 but nothing serious.
Length five and a half miles (8.8km.)
Park at the National Trust car park south-east of Fowey by Tregear's Wood 109 502.
OS Map Explorer 107 St Austell & Liskeard
Refreshments Coombe Farm near car park offers cream teas. Limited availability at Polkerris by a short diversion part way round, but this does incur a descent and climb back. Alternatively plenty of choice in Fowey itself nearby. The Daymark is now open on summer Sunday afternoons you might wish to plan your walk accordingly.

1 Exit the car park going back the way you came. Presently a footpath joins from the right the 'Saints Way', continue forward, you follow this 'Saints Way' with its distinctive waymark a Celtic Cross for about a mile and a half. Just after Lankelly Farm there is a sharp left turn off the road.

2 The path descends into a valley, crosses a stream and goes under an arch to climb out of a wooded valley. It passes Trenant Farm crosses a driveway to climb a stone stile. It goes over the hill to descend by a long flight of steps to cross a bridge going towards Tregaminion. At a ruin turn left across another bridge to go up a grass path and through the farmyard bearing right to exit the top gate. Bear

The Countryside Commission as it was then called was somewhat naïve and once went on record 'That there was no proven demand for long distance footpaths'. Since they made that un-prophetic statement about 350 have come into existence! The Saints Way being one of them. It crosses the Cornish Peninsula from Padstow to Fowey and is some 26 miles long.

left up a track to join the road at the top. Here turn right but very shortly turn left on a footpath leaving the 'Saints Way'. As you cross the field you begin to get views of the once important china clay exporting port of Par.

3 This path brings you out on the Coast Path on the edge of a wood just south of Polkerris. Proceed left and south along it. Should you want refreshment turn right and north instead but remember you are adding

to the distance and to the exertion required.

Polkerris is a one time little fishing harbour with fish cellar for processing the pilchard catch, that is claimed to be biggest in Cornwall. The pier dates from 1730s. There was also a lifeboat station here but it was later converted to other purposes.

Gribbin daymark.

The Coast Path then goes nearly due south to the headland known as the Little Gribbin. It then swings south-east for about half a mile to Gribbin Head. This is good high level walking, look across St Austell Bay for views of Black Head and The Dodman.

 The path exits into grassland opposite the huge red and white striped daymark. By all means stroll over for a closer inspection but the better path, currently unsigned keeps by the right hand hedge. This presently passes through a gate and goes down past a wooden seat. At first there is scrub and then a wood. Your ears may well make you aware of the offshore bell! You pass through a pedestrian gate and just before the

The red and white painted daymark on Gribbin Head is quite the most spectacular edifice in miles. It is 84 feet high and was erected in 1832 by Trinity House. Recently however there were fears that the original lead paint that was flaking off might poison cattle. Trinity House therefore repainted it in modern non-lead paint and then sold it to the National Trust for a nominal £1. Quite a bargain when one considers modern house prices!

end of the wood another gate. When you exit the wood go down the hill and slightly left, the path is indistinct, to join the short cut you could have taken from the Daymark. At the bottom of the grassland go through a large gate to join a grassy lane. This presently becomes a footpath and passes over a wooden causeway.

Polridmouth, close to Menobilly.

5 The Coast Path now arrives at Polridmouth, (pronounced locally as 'Pridmouth'. There is a footpath going left but the Coast Path goes sharp right and keeps along the shoreline. The path turns a corner and the Coast Path goes across some concrete stepping stones which are the division between a small lake and the shore. A pair of swans usually make their home here.

Inland is Menabilly, the house that has had at least two distinguished inhabitants. The first was Philip Rashleigh the mineralogist and antiquary, he was a member of the Royal Society and represented Fowey in Parliament for many ears. The second is Daphne du Maurier the author who used the house as her setting for Manderley in Rebecca.

6 Almost immediately after the stepping stones there is a footpath going left inland. Leave the Coast Path here, the path you want is happily marked with a 'P' for parking. There is a track going uphill and then several changes of direction but the route is well marked. The final stretch is a hedged lane and after a while a pedestrian gate gives access to the bottom of the car park. Do not worry if you miss it you will soon come back to the road entrance.

Gribbin Head

8 Fowey – Polruan

A pretty walk alongside river and creek.

This walk is basically called the Hall Walk and admittedly uses very little of the Coast Path. It has, however, been written up as being one of the hundred best walks in England.

A two ferry walk, outwards Fowey to Bodinnick, return Polruan to Fowey.

Level 🥾 🥾
Length four and a half miles (7.2 km.)
Parking is easiest at Fowey where there is a large car park close to the Bodinnick Ferry 125 521
OS Map Explorer 107 St Austell & Liskeard
Refreshments aplenty in Fowey, a pub at Boddinick then nothing until Polruan.

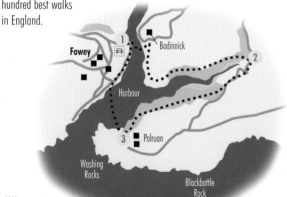

Fowey

Bodinnick

Harbour

2

3 Polruan

Washing Rocks

Blackbottle Rock

1000 m

The Quay at Polruan.

1 Cross the River Fowey from Fowey on the floating bridge ferry to Bodinnick. On landing, go straight up the road passing *The Ferry Inn* on the left. A little further on, immediately after a small bend, you come to an entrance in the wall on the right with a notice 'Hall Walk'; turn in here. The first thing of interest is a Fowey war memorial. Later in a shelter is a plaque. Almost immediately afterwards is the memorial to Sir Arthur Quiller-Couch. The path continues at high level for a while to come out into a field. It very soon turns right through a gate into a wood, no sign at the time of writing. The path then descends through a wood, but watch for a sharp right turn signposted 'Polruan' to bring you out on Pont Pill Creek.

View of River Fowey.

The River Fowey rises on Bodmin Moor and is about thirty miles long, the lowest bridge across being at Lostwithiel. • The house to the right of the landing place at Bodinnick is Ferryside the one time home of Daphne du Maurier. • At the war memorial there is a good view across Fowey to St Catherine's Castle, one of King Henry VIII's artillery castles. The plaque in the shelter tells how King Charles I was nearly killed here in the Civil War. • From the memorial to Sir Arthur Quiller Couch the view is superb and has lengthened to the Daymark on the Gribbin and beyond to the Dodman. Both are walks in this series.

Main street in Polruan.

Polruan shipyard.

(2) Cross the bridge at Pont Pill, note the limekiln on the right. Take the path forward by the cottages shortly turning right up steps into fields. Go through three fields, the first two climbing and the third nearly level. Cross the stile on a path then fork right and after a descent bear left keeping with the better used path.

You come out on a minor road to turn right and very shortly leave the road to go left. Ignore two minor paths going right. The path becomes urban and concrete. When you reach a road, turn right passing Studio Cottage to go down steep steps. Turn left to go along a road to the centre of Polruan and here turn right down to the quay.

The view across Fowey towards Polruan.

Carter brothers in smugglers workaday rig.

A National Trust booklet described Pont Pill as a 'silent private place where old boats go to die'. 'Pill' in fact means creek but is more associated with the Bristol area than Cornwall. • Limestone used to be brought in by sailing schooners to be burnt in the kiln, then mostly used for agriculture or building. • Polruan was once heavily engaged in pilchard fishing and had a sardine cannery. Later it had a rabbitry where you could view exotic rabbits but now there is not even a pastry crust to tell the tale or should it be tail?

(3) Take the passenger ferry back to Fowey to go right and walk through the quaint old town to get back to the car park.

Fowey which has a long and sometimes turbulent history, today is both a china clay exporting port and a holiday resort. One function does not seem to impede the other. Many visitors find the arrival of a big vessel coming up river an impressive sight. • One of the inns in town The King of Prussia, has an interesting sign showing the Carter brothers, notorious smugglers, the elder was the 'king'. On one side of the sign they are shown in rough seamen's rig but on the other in smart suits because they were God fearing men and went to church every Sunday!

Carter brothers on Sundays.

51

A spectacular view from above Polruan north-westward over Fowey. The River Fowey winds its way into the mid distance, with Pont Pill creek seen on the right.

9 Cawsand – Rame Head

A walk taking in coastal forts and a tiny fishing port.

This walk is not far from the urban area of Plymouth yet it is practically unspoilt.

Admittedly the start of this walk is poor with two stretches of road but there is some very good coastal walking to come. A long length is on a one time carriage drive.

Level 🐾 🐾 but despite some climbs this is mostly very easy walking.

Length just under five miles (8km.)

Park at public car park south-west of Cawsand 431 502

OS Map Explorer 108 Lower Tamar Valley & Plymouth

Refreshments in Cawsand but that is the only place en route.

Whitsand Bay.

Map labels:
Kingsand
Cawsand
1
Cawsand Bay
2
Polhawn Cove **3**
Rame
Middlebarton Brake
5 Penlee Point
4
Rame Head

1000 m

1 Exit the car park through the top entrance and then go forward, not left or right. This is a leap of faith because there is no sign to say where you are going. There is a shelter on a grass plot with a telephone box beside it, pass these and proceed. At the first road junction turn right and almost immediately left on to a public footpath.

2 The footpath soon goes steeply uphill, keep with hedge on left hand side. Shortly the slope eases but the ill-defined path continues uphill still close to left hedge. At the end of the footpath you again reach a road. Turn right uphill to arrive at a bend with two tracks going left. Here take the second left, a lane descending to Polhawn Cove. Despite being a private drive it is a

public footpath. A little way down the slope fork right and shortly ignore a footpath going off right.

Polhawn Fort was one of a chain of forts built to protect Plymouth in the 1860s. Fifty were proposed but not all were built. They have rather unfairly been called Palmerston's Follies but he was forced into action by public opinion due to sabre rattling by Napoleon III of France. Polhawn Fort itself was to guard against landings on the shores of Whitsand Bay. It had a drawbridge raised each evening and lowered each morning. It was manned until 1926.

Cawsand and Kingsand are cheek by jowl but until the mid nineteenth century were in different counties. Kingsand was in Devon and Cawsand in Cornwall. Cawsand has a long history of being involved in smuggling. That it was not suppressed may be due to the calibre of those in the Custom Service. A seventeenth century report on the Cawsand official was not complimentary. "Ancient idle fellow set on fishing had never done any work nor ever will".

Polhawn Fort.

3 At Polhawn join and go left and forward on the Coast Path. There is a sharp left turn up steps to get to a higher level. You cross a track and there are more steps. The path then climbs towards Rame Head allowing views west across Whitsand Bay to the south Cornish coast beyond.

4 You do not have to go out on to Rame Head but the walk out was included in the distance and you will miss a good view point if you do not! Look out to sea for a view of Eddystone lighthouse but it must be admitted you cannot always see it, because of poor visibility.

Rame Head.

Rame Head has a long and interesting history. There was an Iron Age fort here and possibly in Norman and certainly medieval times a chapel to St Michael was erected on the top. It was owned by Tavistock Abbey. There is a record from as early as 1543 of a watchman posted here to provide a light for ships returning from the Newfoundland trade. There was a beacon at the time of the Armada in 1588 and defences were erected in World War II. Eddystone Lighthouse is often clearly seen from Rame Head, this being the nearest place on the mainland to it. Let us hope this does not cause an inter-county incident because despite its nearness to Cornwall Eddystone is classified as part of Devon! Both the first two Eddystone lighthouses were made of wood rather than stone because it was felt that a degree of elasticity in the material would better resist the assault of the sea.

After Rame Head continue with the Coast Path towards Penlee Point. The carriage drive is joined at a bend shortly before you reach Penlee, fork right, it is at first old tarmac and then new. If you want to visit the grotto, watch for three wooden seats to the right of the route. About fifteen yards past these there are steps going down to two more seats. Take these steps and then a rough path going down and then left to the grotto. Even if you omit the grotto you have a good view of the Breakwater and Plymouth Sound from the road above. A good point to pause here because many views from now on are obstructed by trees.

The Earl's Carriage Drive was for the great house at Mount Edgcumbe, it served a similar purpose as Lady Baring's Drive at Noss Mayo or the Hobby Drive at Clovelly. Visitors were driven out to be impressed by the estate. The Grotto is also known as Princess Adelaide's Chapel as it was visited by her in 1827. She later became Queen Adelaide as wife of King William IV.

Rame Head from the Grotto.

Plymouth Sound was not a safe anchorage for a sailing fleet when a gale came from the south-west. To obviate this problem the Breakwater was built, a massive undertaking, the Channel Tunnel of its day. It was started in 1812 and took thirty years to complete with 700 men employed at its peak. The Breakwater Fort was cleverly built, detached from the Breakwater itself. This was done to prevent a hostile force landing on the Breakwater and being able to rush the Fort.

Cawsand Square.

(5) The way now turns north-wards and is for a long while wooded. The Coast Path for quite a stretch is a road but just after another seat, branches right on a track Observe the old terrace below the route shortly after Penlee Point. Keep with the Coast Path which is well way-marked all the way back to Cawsand, sometimes track sometimes tarmac. You arrive down a lane to the Square, refreshment is forward the car park is up and left. A little way up the road is an inconspicuous right turn, Armada Road, turn here to regain the car park.

Kingsand from Cawsand.

The row of terrace houses below the path after Penlee Point, now called the Old Signal Station, was erected by Trinity House to provide homes for the men who maintained the warning foghorn. The locals always called it the 'Penlee 'ooter'.

10 Cremyll – Kingsand – Cremyll

A walk so near the city but so different.

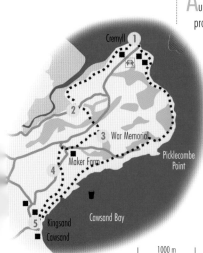

An interesting and mostly unfrequented walk, despite its proximity to the big city of Plymouth. However because Plymouth, incorporating Devonport, has a long association with war you will come across evidence of past defence activities.

A lot of level walking but a couple of considerable climbs one of these being late on.

Level 🌶🌶

Length seven miles (11.2 km.) but the extension into Kingsand will add half a mile.

Start two possibilities. If in Cornwall go to Cremyll and park in car park there 453 533. If in Devon it is usually easier to park in Cremyll Ferry car park in Plymouth 463 539 and catch the ferry to Cremyll.

OS Maps Explorer 1108 Lower Tamar Valley

Refreshments at Cremyll there is a pub and a café at the Orangery close to the end of the walk. There is a restaurant at Maker Farm part way round the circuit. Plenty of choice in Kingsand. If you use the ferry there is a café close to the top of the slipway on the Plymouth side, but be warned this is an early opener but also an early closer.

Cremyll - Kingsand - Cremyll

59

1 If you came by car walk towards the ferry landing point to turn left on to the footpath. If you came by ferry take off on the footpath to the right of the B 3247 opposite the landing point. The start is just to the left of a telephone box and is signed 'Empacombe ¾ '. In a few yards there is an unmarked junction go left. At the next signed junction right. Note the obelisk soon high up to your left.

The footpath goes along close to the shore line to come to Empacombe. Here you go down a short drive and then on to a lawn to turn left around the little harbour side. The route then continues along the shoreline past Painter Point to meet a minor road.

Obelisk to a pet pig.

Cremyll Ferry.

The Tamar is 50 miles long and now provides practically all of the boundary between Devon and Cornwall. It was once, when mining was in its heyday, a great inland trade route. Cremyll has the same root as the Kremlin in Moscow. It is a Scandinavian word meaning a strong place, in other words a fortified hill at the mouth of the Tamar. • Part of the ferry ticket office was once a toll house for collecting fares from those using the old carriage road into Cornwall. Its inscription might be the spur to start your walk it reads 'Does thou love life? Then do not squander time!' • The obelisk was erected by a Countess Mt Edgecumbe, could it be said with aristocratic eccentricity, in memory of a pet pig! • Empacombe was where the second Eddystone Lighthouse was assembled. It operated from 1709 to 1755 when it was burnt down.

Empacombe.

(2) Cross this road to pick up a footpath practically opposite going into a field. Here take care; the obvious grass track on the left side of the field is NOT the way you want. After just a few yards, before the first bend on the track the footpath swings right, away from the track and heads for the top of the field. At the top of the field the path enters a wood through a kissing gate and climbs steeply in a series of zigzags. At one point you cross a track to go up stone steps opposite to come to the 'B' road. Cross this and go ahead to cross another road to get to Maker Church.

Maker church is dedicated to St Julian the patron saint of ferrymen. It was the scene of a murder once when a night watchman was killed. A man from Saltash was later arrested brought to trial and hanged at Exeter.

(3) The footpath turns right into a field opposite the church entrance, keeping by left hand hedge. It comes to a stile where you can turn back for good view of the Tamar. The path continues through fields and then enclosed to come to Maker Farm. Here cross a track to continue through fields to reach a road. Turn right and fork right at the road junction. Turn left on to a footpath just before an acute bend in the road. The path in the next long field goes straight across the field roughly parallel to but away from the hedge line. There are good views to your left of Plymouth Sound, the Breakwater and the Mewstone off Wembury beyond. This path comes out on yet another road which you need to cross to continue.

Old county boundary.

(4) Pick up the high level path which descends past old fortifications. In a very few yards, on the right, note the first of a series of WD War Department marker stones. Ignore a footpath going off left to come eventually to a four-way footpath crossroads. Two are signed for 'Kingsand', the left turn is the one you want. The path descends steeply and becomes a road which you presently find, watching to your left, called Devonport Hill'. A very few yards after the road name is a cross roads and it is decision time.

(5) If well-fed and have no interest in history the short cut option is to turn left and enter Mount Edgcumbe Countryside Park. The hungry and historic proceed ahead down an urban but quite attractive lane signed 'Unsuitable for motors' which tells you its name at the other end, 'Heavitree Hill'. At the bottom turn left go round the kink and come out on the 'main' shoreline road, turn right. Then take the next turn left 'Garrett Street'. The old border marker is about twenty yards along up on a house wall on your left. Curiosity satisfied and possibly refreshed return the way you came back to the entrance of Mount Edgcumbe House Countryside Park.

The Orangery Gardens Mount Edgecumbe.

Folly in name and design.

Until the middle of the 19th century Cawsand, the adjoining village, was in Cornwall but Kingsand in Devon. The reason for this goes back a thousand years to times when the Vikings were a threat. They had a habit of coming into estuaries looking for rich pickings from poorly defended areas. The Saxon authorities tried to counter this by seeing that both sides of a river mouth were under a single control.

The path soon becomes the Coast Path so you only have to follow the waymarks and acorns to Cremyll. After about a mile there is a short stretch of road, when the path leaves this road it goes sharp right. It then goes uphill and begins a long stretch of woodland. Note the unusual summer house on your left at a bend in the path. Unfortunately due to a landslip there is a big climb turn left after a large stone basin, no mark here at time of writing. Watch out for deer they can surprise you! A yard or two before a wooden causeway look right for view of Drake's Island. The path rises briefly into more open land, look for the folly tower up to your left. Keep right to re-enter woodland which is left by a Greek Temple summer house. Walk through open grassland at Barn Pool. The route passes by the gardens of Mount Edgecumbe to come to the Orangery. Continue on from here to leave the park and come to the car park or ferry point.

View coming to Barn Pool.

'Temple' near Barn Pool.

The summer house on the bend is part of a 're-cycled' church from Plymouth. • Drake's island was used as a prison after the Civil war and fortified as late as World War II. • The folly tower was built as a 'ruin', this may seem a strange idea to us but it was once a vogue to add character when laying out an estate. • Barn Pool looks peaceful now but was one of the busy embarkation points for American forces before 'D' Day. • The Mount Edgcumbe family prospered so they moved down the Tamar from Cotehele to build a new house in their deer park near the river mouth. The Duke of Medina Sidonia was a guest there and thought it might make a suitable English residence for himself. Unfortunately for him his 'team', the Armada, lost their 'away match' so he never had the opportunity! • In World War II the big house was destroyed by incendiary bombs but rebuilt afterwards.